The Weird One

By

Michael Scott

I'm living the dream baby. Living the dream- Big Mike

Table of Contents

Dedication

Introduction

Chapter 1

Chapter 2

Chapter 3

Chapter 4

Chapter 5

Chapter 6

Dedication

I want to take this second to thank a bunch of people and dedicate this book to them. My Mom and my Dad thank you for giving birth to me mighty appreciated. To my wife Tiff and my kids Nick, Diana, Devan, Isaiah. I love you guys and thanks for being my world and for always loving me. I also can't forget my in laws. My mother in law Jean and my sister's and brother in law

Linda, Danny and Deb, to you Thank you for being in my life I love you all.

Most importantly to God for allowing the opportunities that I have had that this book is made of. Thank you for always loving me and never leaving nor forsaking me.

I also would like to dedicate this to my heroes. The people I admire. First off my little brother Joe who constantly is protecting our freedom as Americans and to my sister in law Crystal and all Nieces and Nephews I love you all. Never be afraid to live your dreams.   To my friends of over 30 years Steve Cyphers, Crystal Coker, and my birthday twins Wendy and Robbie Jennings.

I love you guys and thanks for being my friend all these years. Wrestling personality and legend Bill Apter. Thanks for giving me the idea to write these things. Believe it or not that phone conversation helped both of us.

To my wrestling family Jay Cortez, Shawn Hardy, Shawn Carlson, and Steve Coleman (you son of a....), Matt Wylde, Ryan Vox,

Kory Cross Aaron Stewart, Ashley Bergold, Yams the working man and Eric Nelson. I love you guys. Thank you for being my friends and always wanting what's best for me.

To all my acting friends. Lisa Tobias and Catrine, Aynsleigh Pollarine, Latice Klappa and Mike Lemon.

Thanks guys for supporting me in what I've done.

To all of you this book is dedicated to each

and every one of you.

Introduction

Hello Friends and Neighbors. I say that because if you read this you are a friend and in the digital age we are all neighbors I suppose. So you dear reader may be thinking am I getting myself into a horror book with the name that I chose and the answer is NO. This book is about my life. Now mind you I know I'm not famous and I know it isn't very long for the shear fact that I'm not dead and I have a whole lot of living left to do after this book's been written.

I hope that you take one thing out of this book. That is something very simple and easy. You can do ANYTHING!!!! I'm not talking some things. I'm not talking most things. I'm talking ANYTHING!!!! The power to change your life is in your hands. You have those choices daily. Trust me I make these choices on a daily basis. I'm not going to preach to you about all this stuff. I'll leave that for the televangelists of the world. I'm going to shoot straight and tell you the truth. Now I will say this some things have been omitted because I don't want to get sued for dropping names.

I ain't got time for dat. So sit back, relax, have a nice up of coffee and enjoy my story.

Hopefully you can learn something from it and will not make the same mistakes I made. Read the stories and hopefully take the things I have done and become fearless and live your dreams. That's what I want for all of us is to be The Weird One, like how I did that.

Chapter 1 The beginning

Let's start way back in the backseat of my daddy's car. A little kissing, holding, cuddling….. You get the idea. I am the oldest son of Randolph and Paulette Scott. I do have a younger brother but he isn't going to want to be mentioned so we won't. I was born August 2, year we won't mention for two reasons. Number 1, I don't want you people to know how old I am. Number 2, I don't want my identity stolen and someone try to pass as me and drive away with a brand new Camaro. I want that damn Camaro. Sorry getting off subject. I was born in the happening town of Warner Robins. We were a regular family. Not much craziness except…Well we won't talk about that. I guess you can say, well no I was a very odd child. I've always like weird stuff such as, oldies on the radio, old movies, old pro wrestling tapes, old comedy videos. You getting where I'm going with this. Dammit I like old stuff.

As I was growing up I had two things I could count on to get me through anything. That was pro wrestling, which we talk about later, and Comedy. I love to laugh and I love to make people laugh ever since I was young. One time I was eating at a fast food joint, I won't mention the name because I don't want to get sued, and my dad got so pissed at me because I was talking to strangers and entertaining. Yep that's me Mr. Entertainment.

This is a running lot in my life I always have been the dreamer. It's hard to say when it started but I've always had grand dreams. I remember when I was a kid and I would imagine me performing doing stand-up or doing something acting related and making people laugh. At 6 ft 2 and 100 pounds soaking wet I was a catch and trust me it's wasn't easy being that studly. I was bullied terribly. Please remember this If you are picked on or have been picked on please remember, "People hate what they don't understand. You're not weird you just understand different things than they do. Psst they are the freaks not YOU." Ok off that soap box. When I was 11 I actually contemplated committing suicide. I remember at one point my whole sixth grade class wanted to beat me up. Yeah the struggle was real. By the way, extremely thankful I never did that because boy what I would've missed.

Trust me if this is you reading this book, Don't do it. It is not worth it. Trust me it may look bleak now and it may look like you have nothing to live for but you do. You have so much to live for that you don't even realize yet.

Think about all the fun times that you will have and all the adventures with people who get you and understand you. You haven't met them yet and it's ok. Trust me they will come. Trust me you are loved and wanted in this world. If you don't think so then I love you. Yep you heard me right. I love you. I know what it is to go through life in the dark and walk around thinking you're the only one on this earth. Well, that's the truth actually we are all created genuine and original everything about you is unique and special. Not to get preachy but... That's the uniqueness of us as humans. We are all created different but the same. Funny how we don't see that so just remember when you think no one loves you... Big Mike does.

Chapter 2 The Church

At the age of 16 I was saved. I can remember sitting on the front pew of that church with my great grandmother and just saying to myself you know what this is a good idea. I became a Christian and when I turned 18 I started preaching in churches. Something about that pulpit really gravitated to me. That was a lot of fun. It was during this time I knew I had a gift for the gab, as my dad would say. I would do usually stuff in our local church but sometimes I would go to my uncle's church and do it. That was another fun little deal. Travelling the state and yes I did it with my mom of course because being on the road alone just sucks and I love my mama just saying. I got to see a lot and speak a lot which was very cool and I also got to touch lives the best way I knew how.

    I have always been a talker like I said before. I've always been Mr. Entertainer. I try to turn it off but sometimes you just can't.

It was weird being 18 and telling 60 year old's how to live their life. Seeing a common denominator here in every situation it was weird and different but the reason I could do it was all because I stood up and just did it. You starting to catch what I'm pitching.

I actually have a very cool story about this one time I wrote a sermon and was visited in the night. Now you can believe this or you don't up to you entirely but I wrote a sermon about having the fire for God. Back then I was like Go Jesus. I still am just a little more fervent than how I am now. But I digress. So I had written it and had it done. I went to bed and had a visit. It was dark I'd say around 1 am, because I was young and could hang with the big dogs back then. I was laying in my bed and something grabbed me I'm talking physically grabbed me. All I said was "Off of me in the name of Jesus." Yes I did sound like a crazy man but I flew up and a peace came over that room. I slept like a baby. You can believe it or you don't your call totally but it happened and I never will forget it. I did a lot of things that didn't make sense and things happened to me that didn't make sense. Years later as an adult me and my friends Luke and Seth went out into downtown Anchorage, Yes Alaska, and witnessed. We picked up a man that was looking for a ride. I was in a small car back in those days. So me and my friends Luke and Seth gave him a ride to where he was going. Now imagine three guys and a bum sitting in a tiny car. That guy pulled a knife on me and tried to stab me. As he reached over with the knife to stab me something blocked his hand from doing that I mean I could see him struggling to fight whatever it was. And then something opened up the car door and threw him out of the car, slammed the door and pushed my foot all the way down on that gas pedal. That's the crazy stuff I'm talking about. I've seen people healed, I've seen people's life changed over the belief of a higher being just saying. Not telling you what to believe completely up to you.

Chapter 3 The Dark Times

Man I have been through a lot. Bullied all through school, contemplated suicide at 11, an ex-wife we won't talk about and everything else in between. It's been a rough life when I was going through this dark time. I'm a man who has sinned a lot. I've done wrong things to people, especially women. I am not a pig now but back in the day I was a dirty dog. I went through a time where I didn't give a good flying leap about anybody. These times were rough. They lasted a very, very, very long time. I can remember a joke I used to say to people. I want to leave my women the way the left me broke, sticky and confused. I have seen the dark side of humanity and have lived in that world. I remember at one point I looked at myself in the mirror and thought just what have I become. Sometimes the light is just about to shine the brightest right after times are the darkest. Funny we don't see that. The only thing we see is this dark room and concentrate on it and don't see the exit sign glowing brightly if we just take a few more steps.

The more you keep looking and try to move through the muck and the dirt to escape you will see the light at the end of the tunnel and that's what I've seen in my lifetime. Trust me it's some freaky stuff but I have continued to thrive even after the craziness I've seen in this dark time. I know what it's like to be an addict. I know what it is to struggle with your demons. I've done it my whole life. But I will tell you that the battle never gets easier it just gets easier to manage. So if you are reading this and you have an addiction problem reach out to somebody. Do what I did get a support team that is on your side and want what is best for you and for mercy's sake stop and get help.

One thing I still have a tough time with is the death of my father Randolph Scott. It still just gets me all weepy eyed and things.

That was one of the hardest things I've had to deal with. That's another one, just like addiction, the pain never goes away but in time it just dulls a little. I wish I was half the man he was and he is always in my heart. I love you Dad.

Even after all the times of failure and all the times of struggle, trust me we all do I do it daily. I have dreams that still haven't come to light but I still haven't quit believing in them. I still haven't stopped trying. They can't fault you if you keep trying and if you keep trying. Do you really fail? Is it really a failure to get up and dust yourself off when you fall and get back on the horse and try again. Is it really failure when the latest thing you thought was right and again it is wrong. I think the answer is NO. There are going to be times where you will hurt others, which I have done in spades. One thing has always remained the same. Jesus has always been there beside me holding my hand. Even in the darkness he is there. I'm not getting preachy like I said before I'll let the televangelists handle that job. I'm just saying what I know. I know that all the wrong I've done. He has somehow faithfully made it right.

Again, not getting preachy but you got to believe in something. You just have to. I feel it is our human nature to do so. If you don't then man you will be missing out on a lot. The cool thing about faith is you can have it and you don't have to tell anyone you got it. I'm not the best Christian in the world. In fact my track record sucks. I've lied, talked to women behind my wife's back, and took advantage of people. As far as people to look up to and admire I'm not that guy. That's not the purpose of this book and that's not what I'm saying. What I am saying is that you have to have something to believe. Even if it's nothing well dammit believe in that nothing. It's funny that even in nothing we still have to believe in something. Just that something is nothing. As I'm typing this, the little man in my head providing me these thoughts is extremely tongue tied and extremely confused right now. In fact I just heard him say, "I need a hot cup of coffee." By the way on a side note if you are reading this drinking a cup of coffee raise your glass and enjoy it. I know I am as I am typing this.

Chapter 4 Pro Wrestling

When I was a kid I always wanted to be in the wrestling business. I have no idea what started my passion for it. It could've been that it was the bond between me and my Dad. He would watch it every Saturday night, Monday night and Thursday night and when it was in our town. You bet your sweet booty tootie frootie we were there hollering with the rest of them.

I can remember my dad, brother and I watching wrestling and during the commercial breaks he would wrestle with us today that would be considered abuse but back then it was just a fun fun time. But as soon as those commercial breaks were over we would stop watch wrestling and when the next commercial break came on….Yep you guessed it we would be wrestling again.

I can remember me and my friend Robbie Jennings wanting to be the next tag team champions. Man we had it set up. We were going to Michigan and say we were brothers and the whole nine yards. Yeah, that never happened. I can remember day dreaming about the crowd cheering as I walk out into the hometown crowd going into the cage and defending the world title. That's the dream I've always dreamed. I got to do that, well not defend a world title, but I did get to defend my family's honor and my legacy Dec 9,2017. Yeah it took about twenty years but if you dream hard enough and believe and continue to daydream. At some point those dreams will come true.

    At the age of 25 I got my shot to be a part of pro wrestling. Man, that was a long time ago. That's a funny story to how that happened. I was working for a radio station selling advertisements and had the crazy idea to bring wrestling back to my hometown and somehow work the radio station I was working at in on it. I had met a few different promoters and then got word about AWN in Fort Valley. I reached out to the owner at the time Mike Bullard and he invited me to come and do a guest ring announcer thing for him and that was that. After AWN I met my beautiful wife Tiffany, moved to Delaware and my wrestling career skyrocketed. I worked for many different promotions, ring announced for different promotions all over the United States. I started my own podcast, hosted Q and A seminars with legends in pro wrestling at the world's largest wrestling convention and even hosted my dear friend Bill Apter's One Man Show two times and one of those times was in his home town in front of his family and friends. Looking back typing this Man I've done some really cool stuff. After all that, 20 years later I retired in Dec from pro wrestling and was inducted in 3 Hall of Fames, defended my family's legacy and honor, helped sell out shows two times, raised money for the children's hospital, see what you went and did Mike Bullard it's all you and Eric Nelson's fault. As I keep saying, I am a man that lives dreams and that is the purpose of this book I want you to live yours. You will fail, hate to say it but you will, I do all the time. Haven't heard this voice on the radio or tv yet but one day you will I keep dreaming and working for it because for some weird reason the universe has always allowed me to do that. I think that is where the fearlessness comes from. You got to be fearless to get what you want out of life, I truly believe that. Can't get nothing accomplished sitting on your coach eating chips going "Damn I'd like to do that." "DO IT!!!" No matter where I've gone and of all the things I have done. One thing never changes, I continually grow. I am better now than I ever was back then. My life is so much better. I have gotten to hang out and call my personal friends people that were childhood heroes of the past. The people I used to root or boo with my father. I get to

call them buddies and we eat dinner

together and things. It's crazy.

Chapter 5 The Actor

As I said in the beginning of the book the other dream I had was to become an actor. I can remember my first role as a kid was in a Baptist church and I was the lead. It was a lot of fun and I think that's where it all started. I got to dress up and have fun. Remember Mr Entertainment. Later on in life I would take acting to a whole different level. I love doing voices so I thought getting into voice acting would be a smart thing to do. My wife gave to me for christmas this introductory class at the local community college here in Delaware. I did a voice for a mock radio spot and I was hooked. Problem was to do their classes it would cost me about three grand. Yeah didn't have that kind of money. I mean who has that kind of money just hanging around I sure as hell didn't. I ended up meeting a guy here in Philadelphia who turned me on to audiobooks. I've now done eight audiobooks and yes just in case you're wondering I'm going to make this into an audiobook as well. I've got to meet some really cool people and some of them

I've bonded with on a friendship level. My buddy Uncle Roy Yokelson, Scott Parkin, Beth Stewart, Tim Phelan, Tom Merkel, Mary Lynn Wissner, Everett Oliver and the rest of the Philadelphia gang. Thanks for continuing to push me and helping me grow.

In the beginning I got scammed a lot didn't know what I was doing but I never gave up. I still haven't given up. I continue to fight and grow. I did get to do some really cool on camera work including being on a network TV show, short film and dozens of plays. I got to play a killer, detective, a dying Indian, an old man and sometimes more than just one person. Every time I get to step behind a microphone, step in front of a camera or do anything like that I just light up. It's one of my favorite things to do and since I'm retired from Pro Wrestling it has become my new passion. See like I always say once you live one dream, dream another dream and then dream another dream. Don't stop dreaming.

Chapter 6 Love

I haven't been a good person most of my life. I've done a lot of bad things. Like I said earlier I'm not the guy you want to look up to and jump on the hero train. I've never done anything felony wise but just morally bad judgments, but I just got to say Thank God for my wife Tiffany. She literally saved my life. She just doesn't know how much. I was on a down-hill slope. But she watches after me and keeps me on track and is my voice of reasoning. Let me tell you the story of how we met. It was because of pro wrestling believe it or not. She was friends with a man I am still dear friends with Eric Nelson. Eric and I were at his job discussing wrestling stuff when he pulled this woman on his MYSPACE page, yep I said MYSPACE is that even a thing now anywho. He showed me her and I still remember the picture she had on a black shirt and jeans and her hands were on her hips and her butt was sticking to the side looking might sassy and fine. I looked at her and said "She's hot" Next thing I know I got a phone being shoved in my face and it's her on the other end of the line. She flew me up here and I went back to my job that Monday and gave my notice. That was over eleven years ago. She has taken a backseat a lot and sat on the sidelines while I do my thing but through all that she still loves me. Hell the title of the book is what she calls me. So for that baby doll Thanks. I appreciate it and you are as fine now as you were the first time I saw you on MYSPACE. Oh before I forget one more thing. You can't do this alone. You need friends to help you through. To my friends reading this book I love you all and thanks for always being my inspiration.

I do have to tell a story that I'm extremely proud of. I am also an ordained minister. When my daughter and son in law were getting married they knew this. They called to check it out with the state to make sure if I married them it was legal and it was so they asked me if I could marry them. Not only did I get to marry her and her husband but I also got to help give her away. I am extremely proud of that day and every day that I get to do those things with my kids means the world. Like the time I took my son's Nick and Isaiah to California for an animation conference. We had a blast and them going to the airport and getting on a plane for the first time was a lot of fun to. Those are the things you remember forever. Thanks guys for allowing me to be a part of your lives.

Chapter 7 The Future

In this book you have learned a lot of things. You have looked at my life and hopefully said to yourself "Self, Yeah don't do that. But also don't be scared to venture out and try that new thing you've always wanted to try."

That is my future I think there are some things that I've always wanted to do that I haven't done yet. Like stand-up comedy. I haven't fully done that I've ventured out did a couple of open mic nights but never really tried. I also have always wanted to record an album. I think I'm a pretty good singer and other people have commented on my singing. I figure as long as someone doesn't scream, "Will someone please shoot that dog!" I'm doing ok and I'd like to try that don't need to go on tour or anything but just do a couple of local spot shows on a Saturday night say I did it and move on.

At some point I want to be able to have a Florida house and live my life with family and grandchildren in Florida taking my old tired butt to the beach and becoming a beach bum. Drinking a beer with the world's richest mouse and saying "Yep I can't believe I did that." That's the way I live my life. In fact I will go one step further. What's your dream? Tweet your dream using the #TheWeirdOne and my twitter handle @bigmikescott1 and tell me your dream. You can also go to my Facebook page Big Mike Scott and post there to and we all will be accountable to each other. We all should be Living the Dream. Let's all connect and make the world more daring and more fearless. Just so everyone reading this knows I'm scared to death of heights and rollercoasters so yeah I won't be that fearless that's just nuts. I'll stay on the ground and change the world.

The people wanting to fly and skydive and stuff like that yeah…NO.

Chapter 8 The Conclusion

All my books are short. I just have a short attention span and love the fact that I can write these quick and it's something you all can enjoy. There are three things you need most in life. Number One Good friends, I have that going for me in spades. People you can connect and trust and have fun stories with unless you're in vegas and get arrested then you can't tell those stories. Number 2 is a good woman's love. My wife Tiffany is my ying to my yang. I love her very much. I know I take her for granted sometimes and to be completely honest we all take our spouses for granted. But the bottom of the line is no matter what happens and no matter what is done she is my rock and my anchor. I love ya baby.

The third thing is trust in God and you will win the race. He is the author and finisher of our faith the bible says. So better keep betting on the winning horse. Never let anyone tell you that you're not good enough, talented enough, pretty enough or by all means not smart enough. You tell them from me, if this fat redneck can do it. There's no way you can't. Keep following your heart and never forget to live your dreams. When you lived your dreams dream some more. Never stop dreaming.

If you do that you will continue to live the adventure. I think that's the challenge. Life is an adventure so just go with the what you know and walk the walk, talk the talk and watch you fly, fly, fly

Remember to always strive to be The Weird one and when you do one day the haters won't be standing in front of you they will be standing behind you.

If I can do it so can you. Keep pushing, Keep moving, Keep fighting and you will get to the top of the mountain and yell down to the ground. "I told you. I told you. I'm living my dream and there isn't a damn thing you can do about it."

My prayer for you is when you die and your family remembers you. They will say "Wow, insert your name here, What a Wonderful Concept."

More Stories

I thought these few funny stories would make you laugh a little bit and prove the power of love. I mean it is my book and I am a weird one so enjoy.

Sassy Pants

A few years ago I was going to West Virginia an awful lot. I usually travelled with a few other wrestlers. One of these trips had me, Aaron Stewart and Danny Horne. We always stayed at the same spot. Across the street was a steakhouse that always had great food. Aaron had driven up by himself in the midget mobile, it was a very small car and his big frame driving it is hilarious to see. Well I am a big stickler on time, which is a blessing and a curse. Aaron had himself indisposed and was late. So me being me told the waitress to tell the missing Aaron,"Glad you could make it to the party, Mr Sassy Pants." Well she wouldn't do it so of course cash does do talking and for an extra ten bucks I got her to say it to him. Fast forward a few hours after we went to the arena to say hi to the boys and of course we talked about what had just happened. I got dressed and usually pack two suits just in case something crazy happened. But this time I did not do that. So I get in the car and hear a loud rip coming from my crotch. Yep, I ripped my pants butt to bits. So now I'm freaking and stopped at a local store to get a new pair of pants. Turns out in this tiny West Virginia town fat guys don't exist. So the best that we could do is a piece of hot pink duct tape. Yep I said hot pink duct tape. Finally we tell the tale of what happened and one of the referee's girlfriend had a sewing kit. I'm sitting backstage in nothing but my drawers, shirt and tie. I hear Big Mike we need to do a sound check. I yell from backstage. If I walk out there it's going to be a felony and trust me no one wants to

see this.

Florida Fun

I have two stories from Florida that are extremely funny and kind of crappy, you'll get that joke in a second.

The Dead has come to Life

  This story is from my childhood. When I was in high school we went on a trip to Florida. During this trip I took a beach gazer walk after I left my clothes on the beach. I ended up walking 5 MILES!!!! Now remember I'm in high school. I stopped at a bar, yep you heard me right a bar, and asked how far the place where the buses were parked at was. That's when I learned about the 5 MILES part. I figured what the hell. I walked this far might as well walk back. Well about this time a thunderstorm started rolling in. Figuring I looked lost maybe someone would stop and question me like the cops and stuff because I am walking barefoot with swimming trunks on. Then it dawned on me. I'm in Florida. Oh I'm missing a very important part of the story. The bus was getting ready to leave but they can't because of a missing person. Hmmm. Wonder who that was. As the rain and thunder and all came down I hailed a taxi cab lol. So I pull up turned out that my little brother and best friend had been searching for me and guess what they found, the clothes I left on the beach with no Michael. So when I pulled up in the taxi cab. They thought I had drowned in the ocean and were very pissed. Glad I was alive but pissed that this happened. So needless to say they watched me like a hawk.

The Homeless Mans Bed

This is more recent.

This story starts with me and my best friend Steve. Well we got up that morning and decided to have a guy's breakfast. We were in Orlando visiting the world's richest mouse. Decided it would be a good idea to have a guy's breakfast at an all you can eat buffet. I figured I had an event to be at later on that day and figured my stomach would be just fine. So I ate and boy did I eat. All was well all morning not a problem handled my business just like I would normally do. Well I then go pick up my friend Steve Coleman. Two Steve's in one day aren't I one lucky fella. So we get on the road and down we go to the arena. Well this event had a quart of a million people in it. So yeah that was fun. As I'm driving to the parking spot I already paid for my stomach had now decided to expel all the food I had eaten that morning. Right then. It was Evacuation time. So I had to veer off and of course apologize because it was mighty embarrassing. I found a patch of woods and of course had to make my grab ass about to explode run to the trees. So I think I crapped on a homeless mans bed. About this time I hear something walking toward me. It's Coleman who had to pee. So now I'm playing Hershey catcher while he's watering the grass and the whole time the rental van is running. How that van didn't get stolen I have no idea. But we made it the stadium and had a freaking blast.

The Power of Love

The misses and I just celebrated our tenth wedding anniversary. I did want to include this because of all the stories it is the most special. This is the story of the day I fell in love with my wife.

My wife and I had met through a mutual friend named Eric Nelson.

During this time I had decided to play with the idea of me leaving my little Georgia town and come up to where I live now. Ever since I was a child I wanted to be a pro wrestler. I talk about wrestling a lot because it was so huge in my life. So I worked it out to have my first pro wrestling match. It is 14 hours from where I live to that little tin shack I used to be a part of the wrestling shows at. Yep you heard me right shack and man that place was devil butt fire hot during the summer. Making me sweat just thinking about it.

So that woman and my mother in law saw me for two hours then watched the show. We slept and they got up and went back up north.

Yep she saw me for a few hours to watch me live my dream and then back on the road she went. That's when I finally decided on what to do. My mind was made up. I shortly left and came up here where I have called this my home for over ten years. I gotta tell ya. That was the single handed best decision I have ever made and to this day don't retreat it at all. Thank you hunny for loving me.

These are the memories I'll keep for the rest of my life. Oh and one more for my wife who is reading this. Subi Subi Wabi

baby, Subi Subi Wabi.

Made in the USA
Columbia, SC
31 July 2018